Contents

DAILY LIFE
Read here to learn what life was like for the children in these stories, and the impact that migrating had at home and at school.

NUMBER CRUNCHING
Find out the details about migration and the numbers of people involved.

Migrants' lives
Read these boxes to find out what happened to the children in this book when they grew up.

HELPING HAND
Find out how people and organizations have helped children to migrate.

On the scene
Read eyewitness accounts of migration in the migrants' own words.

Some words are printed in bold, **like this**. You can find out what they mean by looking in the glossary on page 30.

Moving

Have you ever been to another country? Maybe you were born somewhere else and moved to where you live now. If you have been to another country, you will know that it can be very different to your home.

Imagine how you would feel if you suddenly had to move. You would be leaving behind friends, family, and many of the things you know. You might not speak the language in the new country. Every year, more than two million people move to different countries. This is called **migration**.

Why do people migrate?

People migrate for many different reasons. Some people move because they want to find work, or earn more money. Others move to be with friends and family who are already in another country.

Many of those who move are children. They have to adjust to growing up and going to school in a new country. They have to make new friends. Many will also have to learn to speak another language.

Migration from Eastern Europe

Nick Hunter

www.raintreepublishers.co.uk
Visit our website to find out more information about Raintree books.

To order:
☎ Phone 0845 6044371
🖨 Fax +44 (0) 1865 312263
💻 Email myorders@raintreepublishers.co.uk

Customers from outside the UK please telephone +44 1865 312262

Raintree is an imprint of **Capstone Global Library Limited**, a company incorporated in England and Wales having its registered office at 7 Pilgrim Street, London, EC4V 6LB – Registered company number: 6695582

Text © Capstone Global Library Limited 2011
First published in hardback in 2011
Paperback edition first published in 2012
The moral rights of the proprietor have been asserted.

Edited by Louise Galpine, Abby Colich, and Diyan Leake
Designed by Richard Parker
Original illustrations © Capstone Global Library Ltd 2011
Illustrated by Jeff Edwards
Picture research by Mica Brancic
Originated by Capstone Global Library Ltd
Printed and bound in China by CTPS

ISBN 978 1 406 22231 9 (hardback)
15 14 13 12 11
10 9 8 7 6 5 4 3 2 1

ISBN 978 1 406 22237 1 (paperback)
16 15 14 13 12
10 9 8 7 6 5 4 3 2 1

British Library Cataloguing in Publication Data
Hunter, Nick.
Migration from Eastern Europe. -- (Children's true stories. Migration)
304.8'0947-dc22
A full catalogue record for this book is available from the British Library.

Acknowledgments
We would like to thank the following for permission to reproduce photographs: Alamy p. 26 (© Andrew Butterton); Corbis p. 20 (© Dean Conger); Justyna Daniluk p. 13; Getty Images pp. 5 (Bloomberg/Si Barber), 6 (AFP Photo/A. Majeed), 8 (AFP Photo/Marek Druszcz), 11 (Princess Diana Archive/Jayne Fincher), 12 (Bloomberg/John Guillemin), 15 (AFP Photo/Patrick Baz), 21 (Bloomberg/Graham Barclay), 24 (Isifa/Hana Kalvachova), 25 (Christopher Furlong), 27 (Hulton Archive/Topical Press Agency); Museum of London p. 23 (John Chase); Reuters pp. 16 (© STR New), 17; Shutterstock p. 19 (© Birute Vijeikiene).

Cover photograph of a boy dressed in the national colours of Poland reproduced with permission of Rex Features (Sipa Press).

We would like to acknowledge the following sources of material: pp. 8–13 from "No Way Back Where", *From There to Where: Sixteen True Tales of Immigration to Britain* by Marek Kazmierski (Penguin, 2008); pp. 14–16 from *Why Do They Have to Fight? Refugee Children's Stories from Bosnia, Kurdistan, Somalia and Sri Lanka* by Jill Rutter and Mario Candappa (Refugee Council, London, 1998); pp. 18–21 from the Moving Here Stories website, http://www.movinghere.org.uk/stories/stories.asp?projectNo=5. Accessed on 22 November 2010; pp. 22–25 from *Guide to the Peoples of Europe* edited by Felipe Fernandes-Arnesto (Times Books, 1994) and the Refugee Stories website, http://www.refugeestories.org/do-you-live-in-a-caravan. Accessed on 22 November 2010.

We would like to thank Professor Sarah Chinn for her invaluable help in the preparation of this book.

Many people come to the UK from other countries to work on farms. These people are picking vegetables.

Other reasons for migration

Often people migrate because they can no longer live in their own country. Their lives may be in danger because of war. In some countries, people can be put in prison just for disagreeing with the **government**.

People who have to leave their own country are called **refugees**. They may ask to stay in a new country to keep them safe. This is called asking for **asylum**, and these people are called **asylum seekers**.

These refugees are from Afghanistan. They had to move to Pakistan because of a war in their own country.

Migration from Eastern Europe

Since 2004 many of the countries of Eastern Europe (see map) have joined the **European Union (EU)**. The United Kingdom is also a member of the EU. Countries of the EU work together. People from one country are free to move to any other country in the EU. Many people have moved to the UK from countries in Eastern Europe, such as Poland.

This book will tell the stories of some of the children who have migrated to the UK from Eastern Europe. We will discover why they moved to the UK and what they found when they got there.

This map shows the countries of Eastern Europe. Countries coloured orange are members of the European Union.

Poland: 1980s

Poland is very different now from the way it was in the early 1980s. At that time, it had a **communist** government. The government stopped people from moving to other countries. People were also not allowed to say anything bad about their leaders.

In 1981 many of Poland's people were trying to change the way Poland was run. Marek Kazmierski's mother was one of these people. Others tried to start a new life elsewhere. Marek's father left Poland for London in 1981.

These people were protesting against the Polish government in 1981.

DAILY LIFE

Life in Warsaw, the capital of Poland, was hard during the 1980s. Food and other goods were **rationed**. The government listened to people's phone calls and controlled what was on the TV and radio.

Marek was eight years old when his father moved to the United Kingdom. Marek remembers that his childhood in Warsaw was happy. Sometimes he would receive exciting packages from London. Items such as jeans or even soft toilet paper were impossible to buy in Poland.

Many Eastern European countries were ruled by communist governments until 1989.

9

Leaving for London

People need a **passport** to leave one country and enter another one. In 1985 Marek and his mother and sister managed to get passports. They left for London. They didn't know if they would ever see Poland, their family, or friends again.

The well-stocked shops and bright colours of London were very different from what the family had left behind. They found life difficult without the support of relatives and friends.

Twelve-year-old Marek could not attend school until he had learned some English. He and his sister learned what they could from TV programmes. They also went to a **language unit** for children who didn't speak English.

NUMBER CRUNCHING

Poles have migrated to the UK at different times in history. Many Poles moved to the UK at the time of **World War II**, when Poland was invaded by Germany and the **Soviet Union**. Since Poland joined the European Union in 2004, more than 500,000 Poles have moved to the UK, although many have now returned home.

This photo was taken in London in 1985. London is full of people and cultures from around the world. This was very different from Poland in the 1980s.

Going to school

Settling into school can be difficult for anyone. It is worse if you don't speak much English. When his family moved across London, Marek asked to stay at the school where he had made friends. This meant cycling across London every day to get to school, but it was better than trying to settle into another school.

As Marek was growing up in London, Poland was changing. Marek was unsure about returning. He was worried that the country he remembered from his childhood would have changed too much. He went back to visit in 1995 and moved to Warsaw for two years in 2000.

People in Poland are now free to do and say what they want. There is a wide range of food in the supermarkets. Life has changed a lot since 1981.

Marek Kazmierski

Marek Kazmierski started working in various jobs while he was still at school in London. He now divides his time between Warsaw and the UK. Marek has done various jobs, including teaching, and is an award-winning writer.

On the scene

"Being who I am, born in Poland, matured in England, I believe myself to be the best of both worlds."

    Marek Kazmierski

Bosnia-Herzegovina: 1992

Fadil was born in what is now Bosnia-Herzegovina. His family are **Muslims**. Between 1992 and 1995, Bosnia fought to be **independent** of Yugoslavia. More than 150,000 people died in a war between Bosnian Muslims and Bosnian **Serbs**. The Serbs were supported by the army of Yugoslavia.

During the 1990s, Yugoslavia became six separate countries. Many people became refugees in the wars that followed.

Fadil's village was captured by the Bosnian Serb army. His father was taken prisoner. Fadil and his mother, brother, and sister had to leave their home, only taking things they could carry. They became refugees. They travelled on lorries to nearby Croatia.

More than 3 million people had to leave their homes during the war in Bosnia-Herzegovina. Many of these people moved to other countries and became refugees.

Finding Fadil's father

First they tried to find Fadil's father. They contacted the **Red Cross** in Croatia. The Red Cross looks after refugees and helps to find prisoners during wartime.

After a short time in Croatia, the family flew to the United Kingdom. Fadil's father had been released from prison and was waiting for his family in the UK.

Living in the UK

The war in Bosnia was still raging and the family was happy to be in the UK. They still had many problems to deal with. Fadil's father was ill and his mother could not speak English. Neither of them was able to work. Some of the children at Fadil's school did not welcome Bosnians.

When the war was over, some refugees were able to return to Bosnia. Others stayed in the UK because their lives were still in danger, or because someone else had taken their homes.

Refugees often arrive with only a few clothes and other things they can carry. They need help to start life in a new country.

On the scene

Fadil did not speak English when he came to the UK. This made it difficult to make friends at school.

> *"On my first day at school, people spoke to me but I could not talk to them."*
>
> Fadil

Life is hard for everyone in a refugee camp.

HELPING HAND

Groups like the Red Cross help refugees to get to safety. When they arrive in the UK, there are people to help them, including the Refugee Council. Many smaller groups give advice and help refugees to learn English. They also help refugees to meet people from their own countries.

Lithuania: 2004

Before 1991 Lithuania was part of a country called the Soviet Union, which included Russia and other countries. Lithuania became a separate country in 1991, and joined the European Union (EU) in 2004.

Many people from Lithuania go to the United Kingdom to work. They can earn more money in the UK than they can in their own country. Some move there for a few years and then return to Lithuania. Others stay in the UK.

About 3,300,000 people live in Lithuania. The capital city is Vilnius.

Lithuanian school

In 2004 a Lithuanian school was started in Nottingham, England. Children go to the school to meet other Lithuanians and speak the Lithuanian language.

Lithuanians celebrate their Independence Day on 16 February.

NUMBER CRUNCHING

There are more than 240 languages spoken by children in English schools. Many of these are Eastern European languages.

Language	Country	Number of children in English schools
Polish	Poland	26,840
Albanian	Albania, Serbia (Kosovo)	8,350
Lithuanian	Lithuania	4,350
Russian	Russia	3,840
Slovak	Slovakia	2,510
Serbian, Croatian, or Bosnian	Serbia, Croatia, or Bosnia-Herzegovina	2,170
Czech	Czech Republic	1,870

Source: Department for Education, School Census 2008

Memories of Lithuania

Some of the children at the Nottingham Lithuanian School were born in the UK. The parents of these children come from Lithuania and they want their children to learn about the country.

Many of the children remember what it was like to live in Lithuania. They remember the food they ate in Lithuania, such as potato cakes with sour cream. Svaiga was in her third year at school when her parents decided to move to the UK. Svaiga lived in a flat in Lithuania. She expected the UK to be full of big houses.

Many people in Lithuania's cities live in flats.

In some cities, shops sell food from Eastern Europe for people who have migrated to the UK.

Many people who have moved from Lithuania and other Eastern European countries do not stay in the UK for ever. Nowadays, it is quite easy to fly back to Lithuania regularly.

On the scene

"I don't know how to read and write much in Lithuanian because I never went to school there. I enjoy living in England though, and I wouldn't want to live anywhere else."

Kristina, Nottingham Lithuanian School

The Roma

You may have seen stories on the news about **gypsies** and **travellers**. Often the stories are about groups of gypsies or traveller camps arriving in the local area. Gypsies are more properly known as the **Roma** people. They are often forgotten when looking at groups that migrate to the United Kingdom.

On the scene

Look out for stories in the **media** about people moving from other countries. Some stories about **immigrants** only give one point of view. In 2005 many Roma and their supporters complained about unfair stories in British newspapers. They said the stories were **racist**. Newspapers say they are reporting the concerns of their readers.

Ilona Marjanska is Roma. Ilona's family moved to the UK from Poland when she was six years old. When Ilona arrived in the UK, she only knew two words of English. But she was soon able to learn English and make friends.

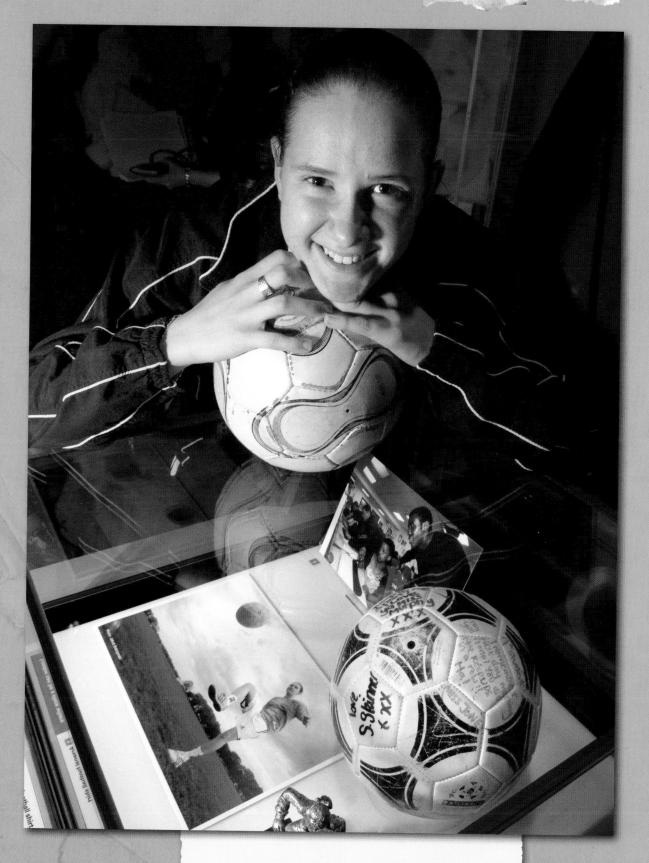

Ilona Marjanska went on to play football for Leyton Orient Ladies and Roma United.

Where are Roma from?

Roma people live in many countries. There are many Roma in Eastern Europe. The Roma often move from place to place. Family is very important to the Roma, and large families will usually travel together.

Roma musicians are famous for playing the traditional music of their people.

One of the reasons the Roma migrate to other countries is because they have been treated badly throughout history. Roma have often had a tough time because the way they live is different from most people's lives. Many Roma were killed in **Nazi** Germany during World War II. They also move to find work.

In the past, many Roma lived in brightly painted caravans like this. Nowadays they often live in towns and cities.

Ilona Marjanska says that many people she meets are confused about the Roma. Some think that all Roma live in caravans. Many Roma now live in settled communities in cities, rather than moving around the country.

On the scene

"I tell someone that I'm a Roma and they go, 'Oh, do you live in a caravan? Do you go out and steal?' And I kept saying 'no' and they go, 'Oh, that's what they heard.'"

Ilona Marjanska

25

Different reasons

The stories in this book show that people migrate for many different reasons. In many cases, people never return to the country where they were born. Refugees' lives could be in danger if they go back to where they lived before. Refugees may be able to return if the war they were escaping ends, or if there is a new government.

People who move to find work and earn money can return to their own countries or move to another one. Some people work in one place for a few months and then return to their families when their work finishes. After 2008 work was more difficult to find in the United Kingdom. Many people from Eastern Europe returned to their own countries.

The streets of London are busy with immigrants from many different countries.

Immigrants have been moving to the UK for many years. Many immigrants arrive with only a few belongings. They hope to make a new life in the UK.

Staying in the UK

Many immigrants from Eastern Europe do stay in the UK. They join people who have been going to live in the UK throughout history. Since 1900, people have come from around the world, including the Caribbean, Africa, India, and Pakistan. Like all these people, immigrants from Eastern Europe bring their own **culture**, from food to music. These all become part of the culture of the UK.

Mapping migration

Some of the children in this book had to leave their home and friends. Their families may have been looking for a safe place to live. They may have wanted a better life.

Marek Kazmierski

Marek Kazmierski left Poland for London in 1985.

Fadil

Fadil and his family were forced to leave Bosnia in 1992 as war raged there.

Norway

Sweden

North Sea

Denmark

Ireland

Atlantic Ocean

UK

London

Netherlands

Belgium

Germany

Luxembourg

Czech Rep.

France

Austria

Switzerland

Slovenia

Croatia

Bos.
Herze.

Portugal

Spain

Italy

Monte

Mediterranean Sea

AFRICA

N

ASIA

Svaiga

Lithuania was one of many countries to join the European Union in 2004. Like Svaiga and her family, many Lithuanians moved to the UK and other countries in Western Europe.

Russian Federation

and

stonia

Latvia

ania

Belarus

ROPE

Ukraine

Moldova

Romania

Bulgaria

onia

Turkey

eece

Black Sea

Caspian Sea

Ilona Marjanska

The Roma moved to the UK from across Eastern Europe. Ilona Marjanska's family came from Poland. Romania joined the European Union in 2007 and many Roma left that country for the UK since then.

| 0 | | 500 miles |
| 0 | | 1000 km |

Glossary

asylum safe place to stay

asylum seeker someone who asks for asylum but has not yet been allowed to stay in their new country. Failed asylum seekers can be sent back to their home countries.

communist political system where all property and businesses are owned by the government. Communist governments often restrict the freedoms of their people. Many countries of Eastern Europe were communist before the 1990s.

culture customs and beliefs that are shared by a group of people, including language, food, and music

European Union (EU) group of countries in Europe that come together for trade and agree on many issues. People are free to move to any country within the EU.

government group of people that makes laws and rules by which a country is run

gypsy word used to describe people who do not settle in one place. The word usually describes the Roma people.

immigrant someone who moves from their own country to live in another country

independent standing on its own. When a country becomes independent of another country it has its own government.

language unit special school for students to learn the English language

media ways of communicating with lots of people, such as newspapers, TV, books, and websites

migrate/migration move/act of moving from one country to another

Muslim follower of the religion of Islam. Many countries in Asia and North Africa are Muslim countries. There are groups of Muslim people living in many countries in Europe.

Nazi member of the National Socialist Party in Germany in the 1920s to 1940s. The Nazis said that Jewish people, gypsies, and some disabled people were enemies of the state.

passport document that proves who you are and what country you come from

racist think that it is alright to treat others differently because of the country they come from or the colour of their skin

ration restricting the amount of certain goods that people can have. Food can be rationed if there are shortages.

Red Cross international organization that helps people affected by war or other disasters

refugee person forced to leave home to find safety outside his or her country, usually because of war or a natural disaster

Roma race or group of people found across Europe. The Roma have traditionally moved from place to place.

Serb race or group of people from the countries that made up Yugoslavia. Serbs make up most of the people in Serbia, but there are also groups of Serbs in other countries, including Bosnia-Herzegovina.

Soviet Union communist country that broke up in 1991 to form many different countries, including Russia, Ukraine, and Lithuania

traveller another name for gypsies, Roma, or any group of people that move around rather than living in one place

World War II war that took place between 1939 and 1945. In Europe the UK, Soviet Union, and their allies fought against Germany and Italy. Millions of people died, particularly in Eastern Europe.

Find out more

Books

Immigration (Issues in Our World), Ruth Wilson (Franklin Watts, 2007)

Lithuania (EU Countries and Citizens; series includes titles on several Eastern European countries), Jan Willem Bultje (Evans, 2005)

Poland (Letters from Around the World), Teresa Fisher (Evans, 2010)

Population (Britain: the Facts), Christopher Riches (Franklin Watts, 2008)

Websites

www.movinghere.org.uk
This website has real-life stories from people who have gone to live in the UK.

www.refugeestories.org
Refugees tell their own stories on this website.

www.refugeeweek.org.uk
This website gives information about events and activities for Refugee Week.

Places to visit

Museum of Immigration and Diversity
19 Princelet Street
London E1 6QH
Telephone: 020 7247 5352
www.19princeletstreet.org.uk

Arrange a visit to your local museum. Many towns and cities have one and you will be able to find out about the people who have moved to your area over the years.

Index